Martin Luther King, Jr., Day

Honoring a Man of Peace

Carol Gnojewski

Enslow Publishers, Inc.

40 Industrial Road	PO Box 38
Box 398	Aldershot
Berkeley Heights, NJ 07922	Hants GU12 6BP
USA	UK

http://www.enslow.com

To Dr. Charles Johnson for his inspiration and guidence,
and to my family and friends for their love and support.

Library of Congress Cataloging-in-Publication Data

Gnojewski, Carol.
　Martin Luther King, Jr., Day : honoring a man of peace / Carol Gnojewski.
　　p. cm. — (Finding out about holidays)
　Includes bibliographical references and index.
　Summary: Presents the history and meaning behind the observance of Martin Luther King, Jr., Day.
　ISBN 0-7660-1574-2
　1. Martin Luther King, Jr., Day—Juvenile literature. 2. King, Martin
Luther, Jr., 1929-1968—Juvenile literature. [1. Martin Luther King,
Jr., Day. 2. King, Martin Luther, Jr., 1929-1968. 3. Civil rights
workers. 4. Clergy. 5. African Americans—Biography. 6. Holidays.] I.
Title. II. Series.
E185.97.K5 G58 2002
323'.092—dc21   2001008263

Printed in the United States of America

10 9 8 7 6 5 4 3 2 1

To Our Readers: We have done our best to make sure that all Internet addresses in this book were active and appropriate when we went to press. However, the author and publisher have no control over and assume no liability for the material available on those Internet sites or on other Web sites they may link to. Any comments or suggestions can be sent by e-mail to comments@enslow.com or to the address on the back cover.

Photo Credits: AP Photo, pp. 6, 8, 12, 13, 17, 20, 26, 28 (inset), 29 (both), 46; AP Photo/Cecil Williams, p. 17; AP Photo/Curtis Compton, p. 34; AP Photo/Doug Mills, p. 36; AP Photo/Erik S. Lesser, p. 37; AP Photo/Gene Herrick, pp. 18, 25; AP Photo/J. Scott Applewhite, p. 38; AP Photo/Leon Algee, pp. 14, 45; AP Photo/Long Beach Press-Telegram, Ken Kwok, p. 41; AP Photo/Odessa American, Cori Takemoto Williams, pp. iii (detail), 44 (detail); AP Photo/Patricia McDonnell, p. 32; AP Photo/Paul Warner, p. 21; AP Photo/Tina Fineberg, p. 40; Cheryl Wells, p. 44 (all); © Bob Adelman, pp. 4, 7, 10, 23, 24 (both), 28 (background), 30 (both), 31, 47, 48; Enslow Publishers, Inc., pp. 5, 11, 19, 27, 33, 39, 42–43 (background); Hemera Technologies, pp. ii, 9, 15 (both); Library of Congress, p. 22.

Cover Credits: © Bob Adelman (background); AP Photo/Odessa American, Cori Takemoto Williams (top inset); AP Photo/Patricia McDonnell (middle inset); Enslow Publishers, Inc. (bottom inset).

CONTENTS

Martin Luther King, Jr., was one of the most important civil rights leaders of all time.

CHAPTER 1

A Land for You and Me

There are photos of famous civil rights leaders all over the walls of the National Civil Rights Museum in Memphis, Tennessee. Civil rights leaders are people who make sure that the laws of the United States are fair for everyone.

The museum used to be a motel. In one room, there are statues of civil rights leaders holding banners and signs. They show what it must have been like to march in a crowd for peace. Another room tells the stories of black children in Arkansas in the 1950s. They needed police to guard them when they went to white schools. In

5

one room, there is a full-sized city bus. Visitors can get on the bus and sit down. But nobody can sit in the seats near the front. The loud voice of the bus driver tells people to move to the back. All these things help us to understand the history of blacks and whites in America.

They show how civil rights leaders helped to make history.

The main area in the museum is quiet. It shows Room 306 of the motel and the balcony of Room 307. A red and white wreath hangs from the balcony rail. But something terrible happened there. It was there that Dr. Martin Luther King, Jr., spent the last hours of his life.

From the balcony, he could see the doors and windows of other motel rooms. Stairs led to the parking lot below. On April 4, 1968, friends and people who believed in what he was doing went there to meet with him. While King was speaking to them, he was shot and killed.

Dr. Martin Luther King, Jr., was staying in Room 306 of the Lorraine Motel on the day that he was shot and killed. Today, a cross hangs on the door as a sign of respect, honor, and remembrance for this great man.

Martin Luther King, Jr., had four children: Martin Luther King III, Yolanda Denise King, Dexter Scott King, and Bernice. The oldest three children are shown here with their mother, Coretta Scott King, in 1962.

Martin Luther King, Jr.'s death shocked people of all races. He was a husband with four small children: Yolanda, Martin Luther King III, Dexter, and Bernice. He was a minister, a thinker, and a civil rights leader. He worked for peace and equal rights for all people. Every year on the third Monday of January, we give thanks for his life and his ideas.

We celebrate Martin Luther King, Jr., Day on the third Monday of January.

Martin Luther King, Jr., grew up during a time when people did not all share equal rights. He wanted his children to live in a society where people of all races could live, eat, work, and play together.

CHAPTER 2

Growing Up a "King"

Martin Luther King, Jr., Day comes each year near his birthday. He was born on January 15, 1929. His parents were Reverend Martin Luther King, Sr., and Alberta King. The King house was crowded, but happy. Young Martin lived with his parents; his grandparents; some aunts and uncles; his brother, Alfred Daniel; and his sister, Christine. His family called him "M. L."

Their home was in a place called Sweet Auburn. It was a black neighborhood in Atlanta, Georgia. Today people can visit the house and see how he lived. It is part of the Martin Luther

Everybody should be treated nice, no matter what they look like. We should love and respect each other.

Martin Luther King, Jr., was born to Reverend Martin Luther King, Sr., and Alberta King. His parents are shown here in 1964 with his wife, Coretta, and his sister, Christine.

King, Jr., National Historic Site. This is a national park. There are buildings and open areas that tell the story of King's life. Two blocks away is the Ebenezer Baptist Church. It is also part of the national park. The church was a second home for King. He would sit in the wooden pews and listen to his father preach. His mother played the church organ.

His father was minister of the church. He was also a leader in the neighborhood. He spoke to everyone about pride and self-respect. At home, he was strict. He made Martin earn his own allowance money. He taught him to work for what he wanted.

Martin Luther King, Jr., listened to his father preach at the Ebenezer Baptist Church in Atlanta, Georgia.

Martin Luther King, Jr., grew up during a time when many people did not have jobs. He knew many poor people. He saw that, in the South, life was easier for most white people than it was for most black people.

His parents tried to explain what life in the South was like. There were laws that kept black people and white people apart. These were called "Jim Crow" laws. They told black people what they could and could not do.

Reverend King grew up during a time when black people could not go everywhere white people could. Some places were only for black people. Other places were only for white people.

Black people lived in different neighborhoods from white people. They could not go to some restaurants and stores. Public bathrooms, water fountains, and swimming pools for black people had signs on them marked "Colored."

Black people and white people had to use separate public bathrooms, pools, and water fountains.

Martin's parents did not agree with these laws. His father asked people to vote for better laws. He spoke out against laws and ideas that kept different races apart. He told his son, "I don't care how long I have to live with this system, I will never accept it." Martin's mother told him not to think that he was less of a person because of his skin color. "You're as good as anyone else," she said. "And don't you forget it."

There were even different schools for black children and white children. They did not play

or learn together. These were called segregated schools. Martin went to a segregated school. He was very smart. He skipped grades and went to college when he was just fifteen. Then, he went to a seminary. A seminary is a place where people learn to become ministers.

Crozer Seminary was in Chester, Pennsylvania. There were no "Jim Crow" laws

Martin attended a segregated school, like this one in South Carolina, where only black children were admitted.

in Pennsylvania. King had white teachers and made white friends. Learning was important to him. He decided he wanted to help and to teach others. He kept studying and became a minister like his father. King also read things from great thinkers who said that it was not wrong for people to disobey unfair laws. He learned about a leader from India named Mahatma Ghandi. Ghandi tried to change unfair laws peacefully.

King thought a lot about life in the South. He had his own plans for changing laws in peaceful ways. His father and grandfather had both tried to make things better. He remembered the words of his mother: "One man can make a difference."

King read about an Indian leader named Mahatma Gandhi, who worked hard to get people to live together peacefully.

Martin Luther King, Jr., married Coretta Scott. They are shown here in 1956, two years after their wedding.

CHAPTER 3

We Cannot Sit By

What Martin Luther King, Jr., taught me:

Martin Luther King, Jr., would get his chance to make a difference. In 1954, he married Coretta Scott. She was studying music. They moved to Montgomery, Alabama, to work for the Dexter Avenue Baptist Church.

On December 1, 1955, a black woman named Rosa Parks was arrested. She was tired after working all day. She did not want to give up her seat on the bus to a white passenger. But the white section of the bus was full. The bus driver ordered Parks to move. This was what was done in Montgomery. When she did not get up, the driver called the police. They came and took her to jail.

Martin Luther King, Jr., didn't want people to be treated differently because of their color. He wanted to make sure everyone had a fair chance to do what they want to do.

Because of the bus boycott that King organized, people of all races could ride the bus together.

Parks was a member of the Montgomery branch of the National Association for the Advancement of Colored People (NAACP). This is a group that teaches people about equal rights. Many people were angry about her arrest. They did not like the fact that black people and white people could not sit together on buses.

Many black people in Montgomery did not have cars. Instead, they rode buses every day. They kept the buses full. But even when there were empty seats in the front, they had to sit in the back. They had to pay in front and get off the bus. Then, they would get back on the bus through a back door. Sometimes bus drivers would drive away before they could get back on.

Martin Luther King, Jr., led a meeting in the Holt Street Baptist Church. He explained that there was not a white part and a black part of a city bus. The whole bus belonged to everyone. He and other black leaders put together the Montgomery bus boycott. They decided that it was time for black people to do something to help themselves. They put signs up that said, "People, don't ride the buses today. Don't ride it for freedom."

Montgomery blacks found ways not to have to ride the bus. Some people drove together in one car. Others walked, took cabs, or rode mules to get downtown. The boycott worked. The black people in Montgomery had come together. Buses were shut down. One year later, buses that separated black people and white people were against the law.

The actual bus on which Rosa Parks refused to give up her seat is now in Dearborn, Michigan, at the Henry Ford Museum.

Rosa Parks was arrested for not giving her seat to a white man when the bus driver ordered her to.

People of all races could now sit together on buses.

Success was not easy. King and many other black leaders were arrested and put in jail. They had to pay fines and go to court. Black people were pulled out of cars and beaten. Churches were blown up. King's home was bombed. But he was very brave. He told his people not to fight back. He told them that the answer to hate was love. "As we go back to the buses, let us be loving enough to turn an enemy into a friend," he said.

For King and other black people around the country, the boycott was just a start. Many groups were formed to work for change. The

Montgomery Improvement Association (MIA), the Southern Christian Leadership Conference (SCLC), and the Congress of Racial Equality (CORE) were a few of these groups. Along with King, they set up marches. People walked through streets singing and carrying signs. They had prayer meetings to teach black people about their rights.

Martin Luther King, Jr., did not believe in violence. He told people that the answer to hate was love.

Students also formed civil rights groups. The Student Nonviolent Coordinating Committee (SNCC) planned sit-ins. At a sit-in, people sit on the floor or the ground to let people know that things have to change. Members of the SNCC sat down at restaurants and stores that were for whites only. They would not leave until they were noticed.

King set up marches to protest unfair laws.

King set up marches to protest unfair laws.

Police officers sprayed water from fire hoses to keep protestors from marching.

Some students became Freedom Riders. They rode public buses through the South to make sure that the new laws worked. They wanted to know that people would let them use lunchrooms and waiting rooms that had once been for white people only.

Not all white people wanted the laws to change. The unfair laws made them feel more important than black people. Civil rights workers were often scared that they would be hurt. Police followed them with guns and attack dogs. They sprayed water from fire hoses to stop people from marching. Some people were killed or badly hurt. There were men, women, and children of all ages in the jails in the

South. Martin Luther King, Jr., was arrested more than 200 times.

Some people thought that change was happening too fast. King was asking them to think and live differently. Others thought that change was not happening fast enough.

King tried to keep things peaceful. Before each march, he taught people to stay calm. Knives and other things that people brought with them for protection were taken away. King explained that nonviolence "is not a method for cowards." He wanted civil rights workers to fight only with their words and their minds. He did not want people to fight with their fists.

Martin Luther King, Jr., was arrested more than 200 times.

Millions of people attended the March on Washington in 1963.

CHAPTER 4
Voice of Strength

ANDREW ALTAMIRANO

★

What Martin Luther King, Jr., taught me:

Remember not to judge people by the color of their skin. We should all love one another.

Martin Luther King, Jr., and the civil rights movement did many great things. Twice, civil rights groups brought thousands of people of all races together. The meetings were both in Washington, D.C., the capital of the United States. The first gathering was called a Prayer Pilgrimage for Freedom. The second was called the March on Washington. At that time, it was the largest gathering of black people and white people in the United States.

On August 23, 1963, King made a speech. The speech was about his hopes and dreams for the future. It was later called the "I Have a Dream" speech.

One of Martin Luther King, Jr.'s most famous speeches was about his hopes and dreams for the future.

Slowly, the government started to try to make things better for black people. In 1957, the Civil Rights Commission and the Civil Rights Division of the Department of Justice were created. These government groups make sure that everyone's rights are protected.

President Lyndon Johnson signed the Civil Rights Act in 1964. It made segregation illegal. In 1965, Congress passed the Voting Rights Act. This made it easier for all people to vote.

Martin Luther King, Jr., won the Nobel Peace Prize in 1964. He was thirty-five years old. The prize is given each year to the person or group that brings the most peace to the world. King was the youngest man ever to win this prize. He accepted the award by thanking the many people who worked with him. He gave his prize money to civil rights groups. To King, the prize proved that using nonviolence is the best way to solve the world's biggest problems.

Television and news reporters followed

After signing the Civil Rights Act of 1964, President Lyndon B. Johnson handed out some of the pens he used.

In 1964, Martin Luther King, Jr., won the Nobel Peace Prize.

Many people followed Martin Luther King, Jr., wherever he went.

King like he was a movie star. There were parties for him. His picture was on the cover of many magazines. Wherever he went, people tried to shake his hand or just stand near him. Other civil rights leaders had been doing the same things that King did. What made him so different?

When King spoke, people listened.

People paid attention to his voice. He was a very good speaker. He knew how to say what many people felt in their hearts. King was a strong, brave man. He was a thinker and a dreamer. He was also a doer. King was always busy. He wrote books, articles, and speeches. King traveled all over the country to talk to people. He moved his family to poor neighborhoods and helped clean them up. Leaders from around the world met with him. They talked about how people of all races could live together in peace.

King knew that if a law or an idea hurts one person, it hurts everyone. He spoke out against war. He spoke out against military weapons. He spoke out against laws and ideas that kept people in the United States poor. He dreamed of a country where everyone worked together.

Martin Luther King, Jr., taught others that differences can be resolved peacefully.

TO THE MEMORY OF
MARTIN LUTHER KING, JR.
1929 – 1968

DISTINGUISHED ALUMNUS
NOBEL LAUREATE FOR PEACE

People will always remember Martin Luther King, Jr., and the great things he did for equality in our country.

CHAPTER 5

We Have Come a Long Way

Do not mistreat people because of the color of their skin.

Today we give thanks for the life and works of Martin Luther King, Jr., in many ways. Schools, counties, parks, libraries, and highways are named after him. His face is on a postage stamp. King's wife, Coretta, helped to create the Martin Luther King, Jr., Center for Nonviolent Social Change. It is near the house where he was born in Atlanta.

The King Center buildings are filled with people who work for things he believed in. There are activities for kids and families. In the learning center, classes are offered for young people and adults. Martin Luther King, Jr., is

Children from all over the country painted a mural at the King Center for Nonviolent Social Change.

buried close by. He rests on an island in the middle of a pool of water.

Four days after King's death, a bill was introduced to make King's birthday a federal holiday. It took fifteen years for the bill to become a law. Some people did not want to spend the money. Others said that it was a holiday just for black people. One congressman did not like what King had tried to do. Black leaders worked together to change people's minds. Three million people signed a petition in favor of the holiday. Still the bill did not become a law. But many states began to celebrate the holiday on their own. Schools and businesses closed on January 15. Workers took the day off. Singer Stevie Wonder wrote a hit song about the holiday called "Happy Birthday."

In Raleigh, North Carolina, there is a monument dedicated to Martin Luther King, Jr.

Stevie Wonder wrote a popular song called "Happy Birthday," which celebrates Martin Luther King, Jr., Day.

Coretta Scott King met with government leaders. She helped to get 750,000 people together in Washington, D.C., to ask for a vote. On November 3, 1983, President Ronald Reagan signed the law. Martin Luther King, Jr., Day was now an official national holiday!

The United States celebrated the first Martin Luther King, Jr., Day on January 20, 1986. There were marches, parades, and candlelight gatherings. The King Center printed special cards with a holiday message. The cards said, "I commit myself to living the dream of loving, not hating, showing understanding, not anger, making peace, not war."

But states do not have to follow federal laws right away. So not all states celebrated the holiday. Each state had to make its own state law. Arizona and New Hampshire were the last two states to do so. Arizona finally recognized the holiday in 1993. Children all over the state let thousands of balloons go to celebrate. It took six more years for New Hampshire to celebrate Martin Luther King, Jr., Day.

Some states hold parades on Martin Luther King, Jr., Day.

Former President Clinton (left) felt that Martin Luther King, Jr., Day should be a day for helping others. It is a good time to do service for the community.

CHAPTER 6

A Day for Action

On Martin Luther King, Jr., Day, many cities and states have services with speeches, music, and dancing. There are prayer breakfasts, speech contests, and peace ceremonies. Schools may have assemblies about slavery and civil rights. King's speeches might be heard on the radio or seen on television.

In 1994, President Bill Clinton made the holiday a day for helping others. He asked people to think of it as "a day on and not a day off." He hoped people would pitch in and help neighbors who need it most. "Every time you give a little," he said, "you always get back

We will be friends and love one another, even if the color of someone's skin is different.

Martin Luther King III speaks about his father's legacy and about standing up for what is right during Martin Luther King, Jr., Day.

more." Coretta Scott King agreed with him. She thought that we should spend the day helping others. Her husband once said, "You are where you are today because somebody helped you to get there."

Some groups choose to remember King by

planting trees, painting schools, or sorting groceries at food banks. Giving blood and cleaning up neighborhoods are other popular things to do. Students at the Manhattan Country School in New York City march each year. The march begins at City Hall and goes through many different neighborhoods. The marchers spend the rest of the day talking about ideas that are important to them. They are learning to be civil rights leaders.

Many children do volunteer work, like landscaping, planting trees, or painting classrooms on Martin Luther King, Jr., Day.

Martin Luther King, Jr., Day Project

★

Circle of Friendship

There are many problems to solve in our own neighborhoods. On his day, think about the people in your neighborhood. Who do you meet every day? Do you get along? What might you do to live together better? Who do you call family? Create a Circle of Friendship as a way to thank the people you love and care about. You will need:

✔ **2-3 pieces of construction paper (any color)**

✔ **colored crayons or markers**

✔ **white glue**

✔ **safety scissors**

1. Trace around one of your hands with a crayon on a piece of construction paper. Help your family and friends trace each of their hands onto paper, too.

2. Use the scissors to cut out the hands.

3. Write names in the center or palm. Make hands for other friends, relatives, and neighbors you would like to include.

4. List ways that they show their friendship and love to you on each hand.

5. Glue the finished hands together to form a circle.

6. When the glue is dry, hang the Circle of Friendship on a door of your home.

Martin Luther King, Jr., Day Project

★

Let's get ready to start!

Circle of Friendship all done!

Safety Note: Be sure to ask for help from an adult, if needed, to complete this project.

boycott—To come together and refuse to do or buy something. It is a way of protesting something unfair.

civil rights—Basic human rights that are guaranteed to all citizens by law.

equality—Same or equal treatment.

federal—The government of a country.

injustice—A wrong done to a group or a person.

minister—Someone who leads religious services in a church.

petition—A written request asking for something to change.

Words to Know

★

race—A group of people with a common background; black people and white people are considered to be of different races.

racism—Treating people differently because of their race.

segregation—To separate groups of people by race.

sermon—A religious speech.

seminary—A school that teaches people how to become ministers.

strike—Workers refusing to go to work. This is usually done to try to get better working conditions.

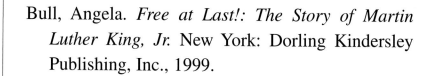

Reading About

★

Bull, Angela. *Free at Last!: The Story of Martin Luther King, Jr.* New York: Dorling Kindersley Publishing, Inc., 1999.

Colbert, Jan. *Dear Dr. King: Letters from Today's Children to Dr. Martin Luther King, Jr.* New York: Hyperion Books for Children, 2000.

Frost, Helen. *Martin Luther King, Jr., Day.* Mankato, Minn.: Capstone Press, 2000.

Johnson, Charles and Bob Adelman. *King: A Photobiography of Martin Luther King, Jr.* New York: Viking Penguin, 2000.

Schaefer, Lola M. *Martin Luther King, Jr.* Mankato, Minn.: Capstone Press, 1999.

Strazzabosco, Jeanne. *Learning About Dignity from the Life of Martin Luther King, Jr.* New York: Powerkids Press, 1996.

Internet Addresses

⭐

MARTIN LUTHER KING, JR. DAY ON THE NET
<http://www.holidays.net/mlk/>

THE DR. KING TIMELINE PAGE
<http://www.pps.k12.or.us/district/depts/itss/
buckman/timeline/kingframe.htm>

MARTIN LUTHER KING, JR.— FAMILY
EDUCATION.COM
<http://familyeducation.com/topic/front/
0,1156,1-4644,00.html>

Index

★